# simple pleasures

# simple pleasures

RUNNING PRESS
PHILADELPHIA • LONDON

A Running Press Miniature Edition™



Printed in China



Library of Congress Cataloging-in-Publication Number 98-68466

ISBN 0-7624-0602-X

This book may be ordered by mail from the publisher. Please include $1.00 for postage and handling. ***But try your bookstore first!***

Running Press Book Publishers
125 South Twenty-second Street
Philadelphia, Pennsylvania 19103-4399

# contents

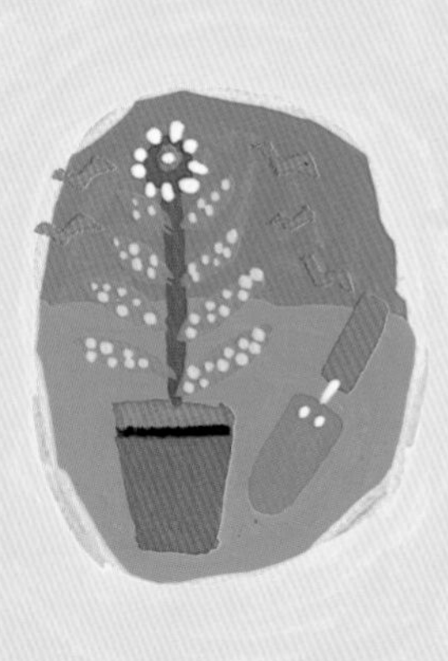

# introduction

Simple pleasures often lie hidden deep beneath the hectic pace of everyday life. Each day includes some pure moment that we should consider ourselves blessed to have experienced. Often, it's the day-to-day gestures of kindness from others that change our perspective on life. Sometimes reflecting on the beauty of nature reminds us of the glory of creation or how fulfilling our lives really are. The sweet silence of solitude may create contentment and bliss. Even in our darkest moments, a memory from childhood or of family, friends, or home, can lift our spirits. Recalling the first time someone said "I love you" can make all our problems fade away. These memories are the simple pleasures of life. Count each one and cherish them.

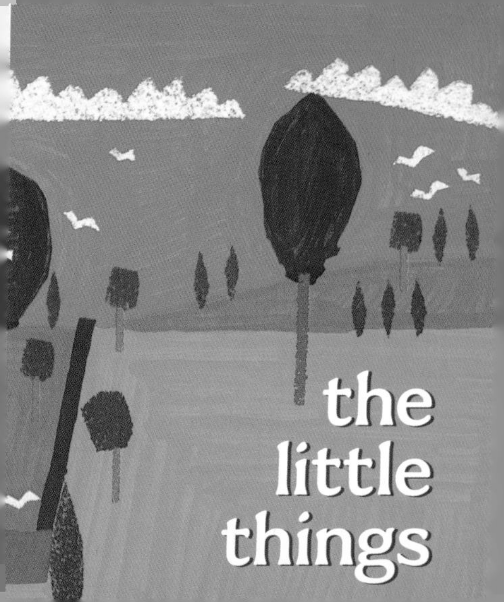
the
little
things

*In character, in manner,*
*in style, in all things,*
*the supreme excellence*
*is simplicity.*

—*Henry Wadsworth Longfellow* (1807–1882)
*American poet*

**Manifest plainness,
Embrace simplicity,
Reduce selfishness,
Have few desires.**

—Lao Tzu (604–531 B.C.)
Chinese founder of Taoism

When we recall the past, we usually find that it is the simplest things—not the great occasions—that in retrospect give off the greatest flow of happiness.

—Bob Hope
American comedian

How simple and frugal
a thing is happiness: a glass
of wine, a roast of chestnut,
a wretched little brazier,
the sound of the sea. . . .
All that is required to feel that
here and now is happiness
is a simple, frugal heart.

—Nikos Kazantzakis (1885–1957)
Greek writer

*Give me books, fruit,*
*French wine, and fine*
*weather and a little music*
*out of doors, played*
*by someone I do not know.*

*—John Keats (1795–1821)*
*English poet*

I used to rail against my
compromises. I yearned for
the wild music, the swift race.
But happiness arrived in new
disguise: Sun lighting a
child's hair. A friend's embrace.
Slow dancing in a safe
and quite place. The pleasures
of an ordinary life.

—Judith Viorst
American writer

Subtly, in the little ways, joy has been leaking out of our lives. The small pleasure of the ordinary day seems almost contemptible, and glances off us lightly. Perhaps it's a good time to reconsider pleasure at its roots. Changing out of wet shoes and socks, for instance.

—Barbara Holland
American writer

*From contentment*
*with little*
*comes happiness.*

—*African proverb*

A hot bath! I cry, as I sit
down in it; and again,
as I lie flat, a hot bath!
How exquisite a vespertine
pleasure, how luxurious,
fervid, and flagrant
a consolation for the rigours,
the austerities, the
renunciations of the day.

—Rose Macaulay (1881–1958)
British writer

He settled into a spot with room to stretch out his legs and he pulled his breakfast from the bag. A ride on a real train. The smell of good coffee. A comfortable seat. He smiled to himself as he unwrapped the bagel.

—Darian North
American writer

*Simplicity is making*
*the journey of this life*
*with just baggage enough.*

—*Charles Dudley Warner (1829–1900)*
*American writer and editor*

*One of the pleasantest*
*things in the world*
*is going a journey;*
*but I like to go by myself.*

*—William Hazlitt (1778–1830)*
*English writer and critic*

*My favorite thing is to go where I've never been.*

—Diane Arbus (1923–1971)
American photographer

*The days that make us happy make us wise.*

—*John Masefield (1878–1967)*
*English poet*

I'm fulfilled in what
I do. . . . I never thought
that a lot of money
or fine clothes—the finer
things of life—would
make you happy. My concept
of happiness is to be
fulfilled in a spiritual sense.

—Coretta Scott King
American civil rights leader

*Everybody has her own reason for joy. For me, it's because I've found my mission.*

—*Barbara Reynolds*
*American columnist and cleric*

We each decided to make a list of the things we really liked to do. The list included things like: Watching a sunset. Watching a sunrise. Taking a walk on the beach or through a park or along a mountain trail. Having a chat with a friend. . . . For the most part our favorite pleasures were the simple pleasures.

—Elaine St. James
American writer

**A leaf fluttered in through the window this morning, as if supported by the rays of the sun, a bird settled on the fire escape, joy in the task of making coffee, joy accompanied me as I walked. . . .**

—Anaïs Nin (1903–1977)
French-born American writer

*Money cannot buy sunsets,*
*singing birds,*
*and the music of the*
*wind in the trees.*

—*George Horace Lorimer (1867–1937)*
*American editor*

There is symbolic as well as actual beauty in the migration of the birds, the ebb and flow of the tides, the folded bud ready for the spring.

—Rachel Carson (1907–1964)
American writer

*It's not a bad life to be serenaded by birds and church bells.*

—*Alexandra Stoddard*

*American writer*

**He was a rationalist, but he had to confess that he liked the ringing of church bells.**

—Anton Chekhov (1860–1904)
Russian playwright

On a clear evening, lie on a blanket in your backyard and really look at the night sky. Gazing at the stars reminds us that there's more to life than we'll ever realize and that every day brings new chances.

—Sarah Ban Breathnach
American writer

I could hear crickets singing
and frogs croaking
and all the other gentle night
sounds of the country.
I felt as though I were in
another, more immense,
never-ending world, and wished
I could keep riding
forever to the ends of the earth.

—Yoshiko Uchida (1921–1992)
American writer

*In March, on those first swooping [bike] rides along the river, there are moments when I think there could be nothing finer than to ride for hours on end.*

—*W. D. Wetherell*

*American writer*

*How many pleasures do we all miss just because we're not aware of them or afraid to try them?*

—*Julius Fast*

*American writer*

**I have a simple philosophy.**
**Fill what's empty.**
**Empty what's full.**
**Scratch where it itches.**

—Alice Roosevelt Longworth
(1884–1980)
American hostess

*Scratching is one of nature's sweetest gratifications, and the nearest at hand.*

*—Michel de Montaigne (1533–1592)*
*French essayist*

*A morning-glory at my window satisfies me more than the metaphysics of books.*

—*Walt Whitman (1819–1892)*
*American poet and journalist*

To own a bit of ground,
scratch it with a hoe,
to plant seeds, and watch
the renewal of life—this
is the commonest
delight of the race,
the most satisfactory
thing a man can do.

—Charles Dudley Warner (1829–1900)
American editor and writer

When I garden, I set out to do one thing and pretty soon I'm doing something else. This meandering—a kind of free association between earth, tools, body, and mind—is for me, an act of meditation.

—Ann Raver
American writer

This fine talent [homemaking] is neglected nowadays and considered old-fashioned, which is a sad mistake. . . . It is the most beautiful as well as useful of all arts. . . . Not so romantic, perhaps, as singing, painting, writing, or teaching, but one that makes many people happy and comfortable.

—Louisa May Alcott (1832–1888)
American writer

*There is nothing—absolutely nothing—half so much worth doing as simply messing around in boats. . . .*

—*Kenneth Grahame (1859–1932)*
*American writer*

*Happiness is the light on the water.*

*—William Maxwell*

*American editor and writer*

**Let your boat of life**
**be light, packed**
**with only what you need—**
**a homely home and**
**simple pleasures. . . .**

—Jerome Klapka (1859–1927)
Russian writer

**One ought, every day at least, to hear a little song, read a good poem, see fine pictures, and, if it were possible, to speak a few reasonable words.**

—Johann Wolfgang von Goethe
(1749–1832)
German poet

For one mother,
joy is the quiet pleasure found
in gently rubbing shampoo
into her young child's hair.
For another woman it's taking
a long walk alone, while
for yet another it's reveling in
a much anticipated vacation.

—Eileen Stukane
American journalist and writer

*Don't hurry, don't worry. You're only here for a short visit. So be sure to stop and smell the flowers.*

—Walter C. Hagan (1892–1969)
American golfer

*Always live each day as it comes.*

—*Gloria Knight*

*Jamaican businesswoman*

*Make the most of every sense;*
*glory in all the pleasure*
*and beauty which the*
*world reveals to you. . . .*

*—Helen Keller (1880–1968)*
*American writer and lecturer*

To see a world in a grain
of sand
And a heaven in a wild
flower,
Hold infinity in the palm
of your hand
And eternity in an hour.

—William Blake (1757–1827)
English poet

sweet
solitude

*Downtime is as important as the time you spend hunkered down doing your work.*

—Maya Angelou
American writer and poet

One of the nice things
about feeling rotten
is having a good excuse to
stay in bed tucked up
with an entertaining book.

—Alec Guinness
English actor and writer

*I do, indeed, close my door at times and surrender myself to a book, but only because I can open the door again and see a human face looking at me.*

—Martin Buber (1878–1965)
Austrian-born American philosopher

*Books, I found,*
*had the power to make*
*time stand still,*
*retreat, or fly into the future.*

—Jim Bishop
American writer and archeologist

I have always felt that the
moment when first
you wake up in the morning
is the most wonderful
of the 24 hours. No matter
how weary or dreamy
you may feel, you possess
the certainty that absolutely
anything may happen.

—Monica Baldwin
American writer

I have a friend who has
developed a special ritual for
getting up in the morning.
She wakes up a few minutes
before daybreak and makes
herself a special cup of tea. . . .
She knew that even if the
rest of the day turns hectic,
she'll have one memory
of something beginning
exactly the way she likes it.

—Elaine St. James
American writer

*Preserve, within a wild sanctuary, an inaccessible valley of reveries.*

—Ellen Glasgow (1874–1945)
*American writer*

My oasis? My front porch.
It's dark, screened, and
partially obscured by forsythia
bushes—the perfect place
to see without being seen.
I can people-watch, listen to
the sound of the leaves and the
creak of the porch swing,
or simply enjoy the cool breeze.

—Salli Raspberry and Padi Selwyn
American writers

*To look for the best and see the beautiful is the way to get the best out of life each day.*

*—Lincoln Steffens (1866–1936)*
*American editor*

I find it wholesome to be alone
the greater part of the time.
To be in company, even with
the best of friends, is soon
wearisome and dissipating.
I love to be alone. I never found
the companion that was as
companionable as solitude.

—Henry David Thoreau (1817–1862)
American writer

**This was the simple happiness of complete harmony with her surroundings, the happiness that asks for nothing, that just accepts, just breathes, just is.**

—Countess Van Arnim (1866–1941)
English writer

*If you want*
*to be*
*happy, be.*

—*Aleksey Tolstoy (1817–1875)*
*Russian writer*

*Life just is.*
*You have to flow with it.*
*Give yourself to the moment.*
*Let it happen.*

—*Jerry Brown*
*American politician*

**It is the chiefest point of happiness that a man is willing to be what he is.**

—Desiderius Erasmus (1465–1536)
Dutch scholar

*Sometimes I sits and thinks,*

*and sometimes I just sits.*

—*Satchel Paige (c. 1906–1982)*

*American baseball player*

*Happiness doesn't depend upon who you are or what you have; it depends solely upon what you think.*

—*Dale Carnegie* (1888–1955)
*American writer*

All fortune belongs to him who
has a contented mind.
Is not the whole earth covered
with leather for him whose
feet are encased in shoes?

—from the *Panchatantra*
2nd-century B.C. collection of Hindu tales

family
and
friends

*Whoever is happy*
*will make*
*others happy too.*

*—Anne Frank (1929–1945)*
*German-Dutch diarist*

*Let us be grateful to people*
*who make us happy;*
*they are the charming gardeners*
*who make our souls blossom.*

—*Marcel Proust (1871–1922)*
*French writer*

So long as we love to serve;
so long as we are loved by others,
I would almost say that we are
indispensable; and no man
is useless while he has a friend.

—Robert Louis Stevenson (1850–1894)
Scottish essayist and poet

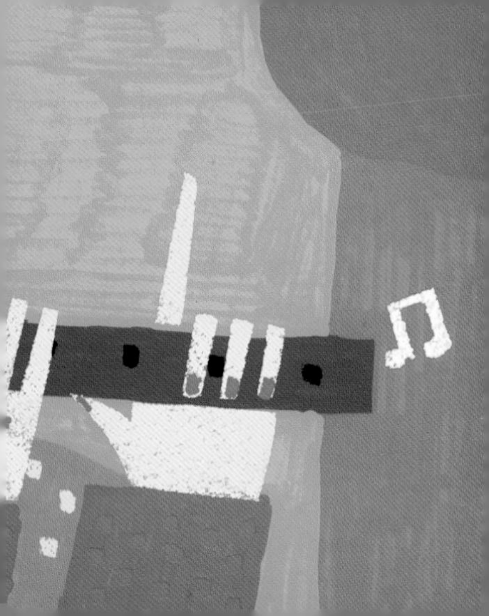

*One can never speak enough of the virtues, the dangers, the power of shared laughter.*

—*Françoise Sagan*
*French playwright*

**For me,<br>a hearty belly laugh<br>is one of the<br>beautiful sounds<br>of the world.**

—Bennett Cerf (1898–1971)<br>American humorist, publisher, and editor

*The most wasted day of all is that on which we have not laughed.*

—Sebastine Chamfort (1741–1794)
French writer

*A good laugh heals a lot of hurts.*

—*Madeleine L'Engle*
*American writer*

**In helping others to happiness we are on the road to the same goal ourselves.**

—Richard Cardinal Cushing (1895–1970)
American cleric

Laughter is wine for the
soul—laughter soft or loud and
deep, tinged through with
seriousness. . . . The hilarious
declaration made by man
that life is worth living.

—Sean O'Casey (1884–1964)
Irish playwright

*I never laugh as hard as*
*I do than with women*
*in my family—my sister,*
*mother, daughter.*

—Cokie Roberts
American journalist

*When you look at your life,*
*the greatest happinesses*
*are family happinesses.*

—Dr. Joyce Brothers
American psychologist

Gradually, I've
come to realize that the
computer diverts
our attention from more
important things: friends,
family, neighborhood.

—Clifford Stoll
American writer

*As long as*
*I'm with the children,*
*I'm doing okay.*

*—Lorraine Hale*
*American child-care provider and CEO of Hale House*

A

It is one of the blessings of old friends that you can afford to be stupid with them.

—Ralph Waldo Emerson (1803–1882)
American essayist and poet

In my country, aged people
have the right to live
with the younger people.
It is the grandparents who tell
fairy tales to the children.
When they get old,
their skin is cold and wrinkled,
and it is a great joy for
them to hold their grandchild,
so warm and tender.

—Thich Nhat Hanh
Vietnamese writer and peace activist

*What feeling is so nice as a*
*child's hand in yours?*
*So small, so soft and warm,*
*like a kitten huddling*
*in the shelter of your clasp.*

—*Marjorie Holmes*
*American writer*

I learned something during my time at home. . . . My kids didn't know or care about how much money I made. They like showing me their art work. They like it when I read to them before naps. I learned money wasn't everything.

—Roger Chesley
American journalist

Whether it's Mama's house,
Auntie's front porch,
Grandmama's kitchen, or
Sister's cramped apartment,
go back to the place
where you are loved,
accepted, missed, prayed for,
encouraged, and
supported—unconditionally.

—Wendy Coleman
American cleric

She sat for a long time
with the brother and sister,
savoring the easy flow
of conversation: the simple
chatter that bounces off
the walls of a house giving it
the dimension of a home. . . .
Skeins of laughter and
companionship spun a shim-
mering cocoon around her.

—Ila Ara Mehta
Indian writer

At the end of life, you will never regret not having passed one more test, not winning one more verdict, or not closing one more deal. You will regret time not spent with a husband, a child, a friend, or a parent.

—Barbara Bush
American first lady

This book has been bound using handcraft methods, and Smyth-sewn to ensure durability.

The dust jacket and interior were designed by Corinda Cook.

The cover and interior were illustrated by David Sim.

The text was edited by Yvette Chin and Gena Pearson.

The text was set in Avenir, Bryn Mawr, and Dorchester.